World's Easiest
No-Knead Sandwich Bread
using a
Poor Man's Dutch Oven

Plus… Guide to Poor Man's Dutch Ovens

From the kitchen of
Artisan Bread with Steve

Updated 10.26.2016

By
Steve Gamelin

Copyright © 2015 by Steve Gamelin

All rights reserved. No part of this book may be used or reproduced, stored in a retrieval system, or transmitted in an form or by an means—electronics, mechanical, or any other—except for brief quotations in print reviews without prior permission of the author.

Now that I have met the standard legal requirements I would like to give my personal exceptions. I understand this is a cookbook and anyone who purchases this book can, (a) print and share the recipes with their friends, as you do with your other cookbooks (of course, it is my hope they too will start to make no-knead bread and buy my cookbooks) and (b) you may share a recipe or two on your website, etc. as long as you note the source and provide instructions on how your audience can acquire this book.
Thanks – Steve

Table of Contents

Note from Steve 1

Two Basic Methods for Making No-Knead Bread 2

Ingredients 4

    Flour 4

    Salt 5

    Yeast 5

    Water 6

    Flavor Ingredients 6

Technique & Tips 7

    Prep 7

    Combining Ingredients 7

    1st Proofing (bulk fermentation) 7

    Degas, Pull & Stretch 9

    Roll-to-Coat 9

    Garnish & Baste 9

    Divide & Shape 9

    2nd Proofing 10

    Score 10

    Bake 10

    Storing Bread & Dough 11

    Equipment & Bakeware 11

- Guide to Poor Man's Dutch Oven (PMDO) 14
  - Background 14
  - Sizes 14
  - Fasteners 15
  - 1-lb Loaf Pan 15
  - Testing the Options 16
    - *Good Cook* 8" x 4" Loaf Pan 17
    - *Mainstays* 8.4" x 4.4" Cheap Loaf Pan 18
    - *Wilton* 8-1/2" x 4-1/2" Loaf Pan 19
    - *American Bakeware* 8-1/2" x 4-1/2" Loaf Pan 20
    - *Lodge* 8-1/2" x 4-1/2" Cast Iron Loaf Pan 21
    - *Chicago Metallic* 8-1/2" x 4-1/2" Loaf Pan 22
    - *USA* 8-1/2" x 4-1/2" Loaf Pan 23
    - *OXO Good Grips* 8-1/2" x 4-1/2" Loaf Pan 24
    - *Granite-Ware* 9" x 5" Loaf Pan 25
    - *Anchor* 9" x 5" (1.5 qt) Glass Loaf Dish 26
    - *SilverStone* 9" x 5" Hybrid Ceramic Loaf Pan 27
    - *Mainstays* 9" x 5" Loaf Pan 28
    - *Good Cook* 9" x 5" Loaf Pan 29
    - *Wilton* 12" x 4-1/2" Long Loaf Pan 30
  - Conclusions 31
- Bread Recipes 32
  - Classic White Bread (PMDO | traditional method) 33
  - Italian Sesame Bread (PMDO | "Turbo" method) 35

Cheddar Cheese Bread (PMDO)...37

Multigrain Country White Bread (PMDO)..39

Beer Bread (small PMDO) 41

Honey Oatmeal Bread (PMDO)..43

Honey Whole Wheat Bread (PMDO) 45

Harvest 8 Grain Whole Wheat Bread (PMDO)...47

Deli Rye Bread (PMDO)..49

Buttermilk Bread (small PMDO) 51

Garlic Bread (long PMDO)..53

Mediterranean Olive Bread (PMDO) 55

Country White Bread (PMDO in a toaster oven) 57

Cinnamon Raisin Bread (small PMDO)...59

Raisin Bread-Raspberry French Toast 61

Note from Steve

The no-knead bread method has revolutionized bread baking. The average family can now have fresh-from-the-oven bakery quality artisan bread in the convenience of their own home with little or no-kneading... Mother Nature does the kneading for you. No-yeast proofing... instant yeast does not need to be proofed in warm water prior to using. No mixer... ingredients can be combined with a spoon. It's almost as easy as making a bowl of *Campbell's* soup.

This is "New Age Bread Baking". I understand what Italian bread, French bread, and baguettes are, and I understand the proper techniques for making those breads, but we live in a new age and we should embrace new ideas. Instead of trying to emulate bread methods of the past we should focus on our goal... to make great tasting, bakery quality, artisan bread with the methods and techniques that fit our busy schedules.

I believe in "Smart & Easy". Note, I didn't say fast and cheap. I make no-knead bread because it's the smartest, easiest, way to make bakery quality artisan bread and I believe my readers and subscribers are attracted to the no-knead method for the same reasons. In response to my readers and subscribers, I strive for convenience and address each recipe from a very practical standpoint... as, I believe, they would want me to develop my recipes.

I think you'll enjoy this cookbook.

Steve

Two Basic Methods for Making No-Knead Bread

There are two basic methods... traditional and "Turbo".

"Traditional" No-Knead Bread... proof for 8 to 12 hours

The traditional no-knead method uses long proofing times (8 to 12 hours) to develop flavor and was designed to be baked in a Dutch oven. The purpose of the Dutch oven is to emulate a baker's oven by trapping the moisture from the dough in a "screaming" hot, enclosed environment. This is an excellent method for making artisan quality bread.

YouTube videos in support of recipe: World's Easiest No-Knead Sandwich Bread using a Poor Man's Dutch Oven demonstrates traditional method.

No-Knead "Turbo" Bread... ready to bake in 1-1/2 hours

The no-knead "Turbo" method uses shorter proofing times (ready to bake in 2-1/2 hours) and was designed to be baked in traditional bakeware (bread pan, etc.). It was designed for those who want to make no-knead bread, but... don't want to wait 8 to 24 hours. Those who want bread machine bread, but... don't want to buy and store a bread machine. It's for those of you who want a fast reliable way to make fresh-from-the-oven bread without the hustle of expensive machines, Dutch ovens, or kneading.

YouTube videos in support of recipe: How to Bake No-Knead Bread in a Poor Man's Dutch Oven (no mixer... no bread machine) demonstrates "Turbo" method.

Advantages of No-Knead Bread

- No kneading... Mother Nature does the kneading for you.

- No yeast proofing... instant yeast doesn't require proofing.

- No special equipment (no mixer, no bread machine) the entire process is done in a glass bowl with a spoon and a spatula... and can be baked in a wide variety of baking vessels (standard bread pan, uncovered baker, skillet, preheated Dutch oven, etc.).

- Only uses 4 basic ingredients (flour, salt, yeast and water) to which other ingredients can be added to make a variety of specialty breads.

Advantage of the Traditional Method

- If you want bread tomorrow. When I the dough is proof over night it is available at your convenience any time the next day... it fits easily into your schedule.

Advantages of "Turbo" Method

- If you want bread later today. Shorter proofing time… bread is ready to bake in less than 2-1/2 hours.

- Some have said, no-knead "Turbo" bread is bread machine bread… without the bread machine. I like to think of it as a way for the average family to have fresh-from-the-oven bread in the convenience of their homes without special equipment or any hassles.

"Turbo" Ingredients & Technique

There are two changes… ingredients and sound proofing technique.

(1) Ingredients

Yeast is the active ingredient that makes the dough rise, thus shorter proofing times require more yeast. As a result, the recipe calls for 1-1/4 teaspoons yeast.

(2) Sound proofing technique

Use a warm bowl, warm ingredients and warm proofing environment. The ideal temperature for proofing is 78 to 85 degrees F, but the typically home is 68 to 72 degrees, which is why recipes generally suggest proofing in a "warm draft-free environment". So, you have a choice… wait longer for the dough to proof or create a warm proofing environment. My favorite techniques for creating a warm proofing environment are…

Oven setting: If your oven has a setting for proofing (80 degrees F)… use it.

Direct sunlight: Cover bowl with plastic wrap, place in direct sunlight, and the heat from the Sun will create a more favorable proofing environment.

Oven light: If your oven has a light… cover bowl with plastic wrap, place in oven, turn light on, and close the door. The oven light will generate heat and increase the temperature inside the oven by several degrees. The amount of heat will depend on the size of the oven and strength of the bulb. The oven temperature will start low and climb slowly. Each oven is different, so check periodically until you are familiar with the nature of your oven.

Desk Lamp: Cover bowl with plastic wrap, place under a desk lamp, lower lamp so that it's close to the bowl, and turn lamp on. The plastic wrap over the bowl will create a similar effect to leaving car windows rolled up on a sunny day.

Supporting video: How to Proof Bread Dough (a.k.a. The Dynamics of Proofing)

Ingredients

It only takes four ingredients to make bread... flour, salt, yeast and water.

Flour
Flour is the base ingredient of bread and there are four basic types of flour...

(1) <u>Bread flour</u> is designed for yeast bread. It has a higher percentage of gluten which gives artisan bread its airy crumb.

(2) <u>All-purpose flour</u> has less gluten than bread flour. I use all-purpose flour for biscuits, flatbreads, etc. In other words... I use it when I don't want an airy crumb.

(3) <u>Self-rising flour</u> is all-purpose flour with baking soda and baking powder added as leavening agents. It's intended for quick breads... premixed and ready to go. Do not use self-rising flour to make yeast bread. To see the difference between yeast and quick breads you may want to watch <u>Introduction to No-Knead Beer Bread (a.k.a. Artisan Yeast Beer Bread)</u> and <u>Introduction to Quick Beer Bread (a.k.a. Beer Bread Dinner Rolls)</u>.

(4) And there are a variety of <u>specialty flours</u>... whole wheat, rye, and a host of others. Each has its unique flavor and characteristics. In some cases, you can substitute specialty flour for bread flour, but you may need to tweak the recipe because most specialty flours have less gluten. I frequently blend specialty flour with bread flour.

Flour is the primary ingredient... if you don't use the correct flour you won't get the desired results.

Note: To know how many cups of flour there are in a specific bag... it's typically on the side in "Nutritional Facts". For example, this bag reads, "Serving Size 1/4 cup... Serving Per Container about 75". In other words... 18.75 (75 times 1/4). That's the technical answer, but in the real world (measuring cup versus weight) a bag of flour will measure differently based on density (sifted versus unsifted), type of flour (wheat is more dense than bread flour), humidity (flour weighs more on humid days), and all the other variables life and nature have to offer. Thus, there is no single correct answer, but for practical purposes... figure a 5 lb bag of bread flour is 17 to 18 cups.

Salt

While it is possible to make bread without salt... you would be disappointed. There are three basics types of salt...

(1) Most baking recipes are designed to use everyday table salt unless specified otherwise. Unless you're experienced, it is probably smartest to use table salt for your baking needs.

(2) Kosher salt is excellent. I use it when I cook, but a tablespoon of kosher salt does not equal a tablespoon of table salt because kosher salt crystals are larger.

(3) And, I use specialty salt as a garnish... for appearance and taste. For example, I use sea salt to garnish pretzels.

Generally speaking, when salt is added as an ingredient and baked it is difficult to taste the difference between table, kosher and sea salt. When salt is added as a garnish and comes in contact with the taste buds... kosher or specialty salt is an excellent choice.

Yeast

Yeast is the "magic" ingredient which transforms flour and water into dough. My traditional no-knead recipes use 1/4 tsp yeast... I want the dough to rise slowly which allows the dough to develop flavor. My "Turbo" recipes use 1-1/4 tsp yeast... I want a faster rises like traditional bread recipes. There are three basic types of yeast...

(1) The most common is active dry yeast which needs to be proof in warm water prior to being added to flour.

(2) I use instant dry yeast (a.k.a. "instant yeast", "bread machine yeast", "quick rise", "rapid rise", "fast rising", etc.) which does not need to be proofed in warm water. It is a more recent development which is more

potent and reliable... and why worry about proofing yeast if you don't have too.

(3) Some older recipes call for <u>cake yeast</u> (a.k.a. "compressed yeast" or "fresh yeast"), but it's perishable. Most bakers substitute active and instant dry yeast for cake yeast when using older recipes.

The names on the bottles can be confusing. When in doubt, read the instructions and look for one that does not require soaking the yeast in warm water prior to use.

Water
Water hydrates the ingredients and activates the yeast. The no-knead method uses a little more water than the typical recipe... and that's a good thing. It makes it easier to combine the wet and dry ingredients, and contributes to its airy crumb.

(1) I use <u>tap water</u>. It's convenient and easy, but sometimes city water has too much chlorine (chlorine kills yeast).

(2) If your dough does not rise during first proofing you may want to use <u>bottled drinking water</u>.

(3) But, do not use <u>distilled water</u> because the minerals have been removed.

Water is a flavor ingredient, if your water doesn't taste good... use bottled drinking water.

Flavor Ingredients
It only takes four ingredients to make bread... flour, salt, yeast and water, to which a variety of flavor ingredients can be added to make specialty breads such as... honey whole wheat, multi-grain white, rosemary, Mediterranean olive, cinnamon raisin, honey oatmeal, and a host of others.

Technique & Tips

The techniques used to make traditional and "Turbo" no-knead bread are identical except proofing. Turbo uses shorter proofing times, thus it is important to use sound proofing technique (a warm proofing environment) when using the "Turbo" method. The traditional method is demonstrated on YouTube in World's Easiest No-Knead Sandwich Bread using a Poor Man's Dutch Oven and the "Turbo" method is demonstrated in How to Bake No-Knead Bread in a Poor Man's Dutch Oven (no mixer... no bread machine).

Prep
Traditional: Because the traditional method proof for 8 to 12 hours it uses cool water to slow the proofing process, thus the temperature of the bowl is not important.

Turbo: To insure consistency and assist Mother Nature with proofing... it's important to provide yeast with a warm proofing environment. One of the keys to proofing temperature is the temperature of the mixing bowl because it has direct contact with the dough. Thus, use a bowl that is warm to the touch so that the bowl doesn't draw the heat out of the warm water.

Combining Ingredients
Pour water in a 3 to 4 qt glass mixing bowl (use warm water and a warm bowl for "Turbo" and cool for traditional). Add salt, yeast, flavor ingredients, etc... and stir to combine (it will insure the ingredients are evenly distributed). Add flour (flour will resist the water and float). Start by stirring the ingredients with the handle end of a plastic spoon drawing the flour from the sides into the middle of bowl (vigorously mixing will not hydrate the flour faster... but it will raise a lot of dust). Within 30 seconds the flour will hydrate and form a shaggy ball. Then scrape dry flour from side of bowl and tumble dough to combine moist flour with dry flour (about 15 seconds). It takes about one minute to combine wet and dry ingredients.

Traditional: Cover bowl with plastic wrap, place on counter, and proof for 8 to 24 hours.

Turbo: Cover bowl with plastic wrap, place in a warm draft free location, and proof for 1-1/2 hours.

1st Proofing (bulk fermentation)
The process is called "proofing" because it "proves" the yeast is active.

Bread making is nature at work (yeast is a living organism) and subject to nature. Seasons (summer vs. winter) and weather (heat & humidity) have a direct impact on proofing. In other words, don't worry if your dough varies in size... that's Mother Nature. Just focus on your goal... if the gluten forms (dough develops a stringy nature) and doubles in size... you're good to go.

If your dough does not rise the usual culprits are... outdated yeast or chlorinated water (chlorine kills yeast). Solution, get fresh yeast and/or use bottled drinking water.

If your dough is slow (takes "forever") to rise... your proofing temperature is probably too cool.

Traditional: Because the traditional method use long proofing times (8 to 24 hours) it does not require any special technique.

Turbo: Because "Turbo" dough use shorter proofing times (1-12/ hours) it is important to practice sound proofing technique.

The ideal temperature for proofing is 78 to 85 degrees F, but the typically home is 68 to 72 degrees, which is why recipes generally suggest proofing in a "warm draft-free environment". So, you have a choice... wait longer or create a warm proofing environment. My favorites are...

Oven setting: If your oven has a setting for proofing (80 degrees F)... use it.

Direct sunlight: Cover bowl with plastic wrap, place in direct sunlight, and the heat from the Sun will create a favorable proofing environment.

Oven light: If your oven has a light... cover bowl with plastic wrap, place in oven, turn light on, and close the door. The oven light will generate heat and increase the temperature inside the oven by several degrees. The amount of heat will depend on the size of the oven and strength of the bulb. The oven temperature will always start low and climb slowly, but it may go over 90 degrees F. so check periodically until you are familiar with the nature of your oven.

Desk Lamp: Cover bowl with plastic wrap, place under a desk lamp, lower lamp so that it's close to the bowl, and turn lamp on. The plastic wrap over the bowl will create a similar effect to leaving car windows rolled up on a sunny day.

Microwave: Place an 8 to 16 oz cup of water in the microwave and heat on high for 2 minutes. Then move the cup to the back corner, place mixing bowl (dough) in microwave and close the door. The heat and steam from the hot water will create a favorable environment for proofing.

Folding dough proofer: Commercial bakeries have large proofing ovens in which they can control climate and temperature. There are smaller versions available for the public that fold flat.

Tip: To fit bread making into your schedule... you can extend 1st proofing up to 4 hours (or even more), but don't shorten... it important to give Mother Nature time to form the gluten.

Degas, Pull & Stretch
The purpose of degassing, pulling and stretching is to, (a) expel the gases that formed during bulk fermentation, (b) strengthen the dough by realigning and stretching the gluten strands, and (c) stimulate yeast activity for 2nd proofing.

Because no-knead dough is sticky and difficult to handle... I degas, pull & stretch dough by stirring it in the bowl with the handle end of a plastic spoon (like a dough hook). It will reduce the size of the dough ball by 50% making it easier to handle and the process replaces folding and shaping in most cases.

Roll-to-Coat
Before removing the dough from bowl... dust the dough and side of the bowl with flour, then roll-to-coat. The flour will bond to the sticky dough making it easier to handle, but do not roll-to-coat with flour if you're going to garnish or baste.

Garnish & Baste
The purpose of garnishing and basting is to enhance the appearance of the crust, but it isn't necessary. If you decide to garnish and baste there are two techniques... roll-to-coat and skillet method.

Roll-to-Coat Method: Before removing dough from bowl... add ingredients to bowl (on the dough and side of the bowl), then roll to coat. For example, when I garnish honey oatmeal bread... I sprinkle oat in the bowl and on the dough, then roll the dough ball in the oats and they will bond to the sticky dough. This can also be done with seeds, grains, olive oil, egg wash, etc.

Skillet Method: When I want to garnish and/or baste the top of the loaf... I coat the proofing skillet with baste (egg wash, olive oil, vegetable oil, etc.) and sprinkle with the garnish (oats, seeds, grains, etc.). The ingredients will bond with the dough as the dough proofs.

Supporting video: How to Garnish & Baste No-Knead Bread using "Hands-Free" Technique

Divide & Shape
If you're not going to divide the dough... it can go straight from the mixing bowl to the proofing skillet or baking vessel. If you are going to divide and shape the dough... dust the dough and side of the bowl with flour and roll-to-coat, dust work surface with flour, roll the dough ball out of the bowl (excess flour and all) onto the work surface, and divide and shape. I use a plastic bowl scraper to

assist in dividing, shaping and carry the dough to the baking vessel. Together they (flour & bowl scraper) make it easier to handle the dough.

2nd Proofing

Traditional: Originally I proofed for 1 to 2 hours, but over time I have been baking more in bread pans and found shorter proofing times gave better results. I now proof for 30 to 60 minutes.

Turbo: Place dough in a warm draft-free location and proof for 30 minutes.

Tip: To fit bread making into your schedule... you can extend 2nd proofing times, but you don't want the dough to exceed the size of the baking vessel. If you're using a large baking vessel (Dutch oven, etc.) it's never a problem, but if you're using a bread pan don't allow the dough to exceed the sides of the pan before baking or your loaf will droop over the sides and be less attractive. But, always bake it... it will still be delicious.

Score

The purpose of scoring dough is to provide seams to control where the crust will split during "oven spring", but it isn't necessary to score dough. If you do decide to score your loaf you may want to use a scissors (no-knead dough is very moist and more likely to stretch than slice). Personally, I place the dough in the baking vessel seam side up... the dough will split at the seam during "oven spring" which gives the loaf a nice rustic appearance.

Bake

Baking Time: Bread is done when it reaches an internal temperature of 185 to 220 degrees F. and the crumb (inside of the bread) isn't doughy. Baking times in my recipes are designed to give bread an internal temperature of 200 to 205 degrees F, but ovens vary and you may need to adjust your baking times slightly.

No-Stick Spray: Most bakeware has a non-stick surface, but it is safest to spray your bakeware unless you are fully confident your bread won't stick.

Ovens: Ovens aren't always accurate. I check the temperature of ovens and bakeware. Ovens with a digital readout that displays the temperature as they preheat are typically very accurate, but ovens that say they will be at temperature in a specific number of minutes are not always accurate. My point is... you will get the best results if you learn the character and nature of your oven.

Oven Rack: Generally speaking you want to bake bread and rolls in the middle or lower third of the oven, but it isn't critical. Just keep them away from the upper heating element or they may brown a little too quickly.

Oven Spring: When dough is first put into the oven it will increase in size by as much as a third in a matter of minutes because, (a) gases trapped in the dough will expand, (b) moisture will turn into steam and try to push its way out, and (c) yeast will become highly active converting sugars into gases. The steam and gases work together to create "oven spring". Once the internal temperature of the bread reaches 120 degrees F... the yeast will begin to die and the crust will harden.

Storing Bread & Dough
After allowing bread to cool... it can be wrapped in plastic wrap, or stored in a zip-lock plastic bag, or plastic bread bags (available on the web). If you wish to keep bread for a longer period of time... slice it into portions and freeze them in a zip-lock freezer bag (remove excess air). Do not store bread in the refrigerator. Bread goes stale faster in the refrigerator.

If you wish to save dough... divide it into portions, drizzle each portion with olive oil, place in zip-lock bag, remove excess air, and refrigerate for up to two days or freeze for up to two months. To thaw dough... move dough from freezer to refrigerator the day before (12 or more hours), then place on counter for 30 minutes before use to come to room temperature.

Equipment & Bakeware
Bowl for Mixing: You can use any 3 to 4 qt bowl. I use a 3-1/2 qt glass bowl because, (a) there's ample room for the dough to expand, (b) plastic wrap sticks to glass, and (c) I don't want the rim of my bowl to exceed the width of the plastic wrap.

Measuring Spoons: I'm sure you already have measuring spoons in the kitchen... they will work just fine. If you're going to buy new, I prefer oval versus round because an oval shape will fit into jars and containers more easily.

Measuring Cups: Dry measuring cups are designed to be filled to the top and leveled. Liquid measuring cups have a pour spout and are designed to be filled to the gradations on the side (neither measures weight). Because of their design and a slight difference in volume, it is best to use the appropriate measuring cup.

Note: U.S. and metric measuring cups may be used interchangeably... there is only a slight difference (±3%). More importantly, the ingredients of a recipe measured with a set (U.S. or metric) will have their volumes in the same proportion to one another.

Spoon for Combining Wet and Dry Ingredients: A spoon is an excellent tool for combining wet and dry ingredients. Surprisingly, I found the handle end of a plastic spoon worked best for me because, I didn't have a big clump on the end like some of my other mixing utensils (which makes it easier to stir and manipulate the dough). And when you think about it... mixers don't use a paddle to mix dough, they use a hook which looks a lot like the handle end of my spoon.

Silicon Baking Mat: Silicone baking mats are very useful... I use them as reusable parchment paper (they're environmentally friendly). Silicone baking mats serve two purposes... (a) as a work surface for folding and shaping (they have excellent non-stick properties), and (b) as a baking mat... specifically when the dough is difficult to move after folding and shaping. And I slide a cookie sheet under the mat before baking (it makes it easier to put the mat into and take it out of the oven).

Spatula: I use a spatula to scrape the sides of the bowl to get the last bits of flour incorporated into the dough.

Plastic Bowl Scraper: I use a plastic bowl scraper verses a metal dough scraper because it's the better multi-tasker. I use the bowl scraper to (a) fold, shape, and divide the dough, (b) assist in transporting the dough to the proofing vessel, (c) scrape excess flour off the work surface, (d) scrape excess flour out of the bowl (after all it is a bowl scraper), and (e) scrape any remaining bits in the sink towards the disposal. It's a useful multi-tasker and you can't do all those tasks with a metal cough scraper.

Timer: I'm sure you already have a timer and it will work just fine. If you're thinking about a new one... I prefer digital because they're more accurate.

Proofing Baskets & Vessels: The purpose of a proofing basket or vessel is to pre-shape the dough prior to baking (dough will spread if it isn't contained). Because no-knead dough has a tendency to stick to the lining of proofing baskets... I use common household items as proofing vessels. For example, I use an 8" skillet (with no-stick spray) to pre-shape dough when baking in a Dutch oven. It shapes the dough during proofing, and the handle makes it easy to carry the dough and put it in the hot Dutch oven safely.

You can also proof dough in the baking vessel if it doesn't have to be preheated. For example, standard loaves are typically proof and baked in the bread pan where your bread pan shapes the loaf during proofing and baking. You can use this same principle for shaping and baking rolls and buns.

Baking Vessels: Baking vessels come in a variety of sizes, shapes and materials. You can change the appearance of the loaf by sampling changing the baking vessel.

Plastic Wrap & Proofing Towel: I use plastic wrap for 1st proofing and a lint-free towel for 2nd proofing. Plastic wrap protects dough for longer proofing times and can be used to create a favorable proofing environment (solar effect).

Cooling Rack: The purpose of a cooling rack is to expose the bottom of the loaf during the cooling process.

Bread Bags: I use plastic bread bags to store bread after they have cooled. And they're great for packaging bread as gifts. I also use paper bags as gifts when the loaf is still warm and I don't want to trap the moisture in a plastic bag... it gives a nice natural appearance.

Pastry/Pizza Roller: The pizza roller can help you shape pizza dough.

"I know when food is supposed to be served in a bowl with a name on it."
Fran Fine - "The Nanny"

Guide to Poor Man's Dutch Oven (PMDO)

Simply stated, a "poor man's Dutch oven" (PMDO) is a bread pan covered by another bread pan. The purpose of the bottom bread pan is to shape the loaf into sandwich bread and the purpose of the cover (top bread pan) is to trap the moisture from the dough in a hot, enclosed environment. In other words, I replaced the standard Dutch oven with two bread pan to get the desired shape... sandwich bread.

Background
The primary reasons for using a PMDO. is to shape dough into sandwich bread and control the crust. Bake the bread with the cover on, then remove the cover and finish the crust. This technique will give you a soft crust which is ideal for children.

Sizes
Bread pans come in a variety of sizes, materials and shapes. You can use any bread pan, but a little general discussion may help you select the best pan for your intended purpose.

Small (8" x 4"): The small size bread pan I tested had a liquid capacity of 42 ounces and I found recipes using 3 cups flour were appropriate for the size of the pan.

Medium (8-1/2" x 4-1/2"): The medium size bread pans I tested had a liquid capacity of 46 to 52 ounces and I found recipes using either 3 or 3-1/2 cups flour were appropriate for the size of the pan. When you use 3-1/2 cups flour your loaf will be 16% larger (picture above)... it's personal preference.

rge (9" x 5"): The large size bread pans I tested had a liquid capacity of 54 to ounces and I found recipes using 3-1/2 to 4 cups flour were appropriate for the size of the pan.

Long (12" x 4-1/2"): The one long pan I tested had a liquid capacity of 76 ounces and it is ideal for both long and half loaves.

There isn't a right or wrong size. Think about your intended purpose... then match the quantity of the ingredients to the size of the poor man's Dutch oven. The process of combining and mixing ingredients is the same, but the baking time will change in relationship to the mass of the loaf (thicker loaves require longer baking times). In other words, anytime you increase flour by 1/2 cup, increase water by 2 oz and add 5 minutes to the baking time.

Fasteners

You really don't need to fasten the top pan to the bottom, but it's more secure and stable. My favorite fastener is the standard binder clip which is available in the office supply section of many stores. If the pans don't have handles you can also use silicone cooking bands or food ties.

Binder Clips: I use both medium and large binder clips depending on the shape of the bread pan's handles.

Silicone Cooking Bands and Silicone Food Ties: When the bread pan doesn't have handles you can use silicone cooking bands or food ties. Silicone cooking bands are elastic and will stretch to fit. Silicone food ties are heaver duty and also work well. Generally speaking they need to be 24+"... you may need to combine a couple together to fit around the pan.

1-lb Loaf Pan

There are several schools of thought regarding the size of loaf pans... which is the true 1-lb loaf pan. Some manufactures refer to the 8-1/2" x 4-1/2" loaf pan a 1-lb bread pan and other the 9" x 5".

Personally, either is acceptable. When I was designing batch recipes I found a 5-lb bag of flour when measured by hand is approximately 17.5 cups, thus 3-1/2 cups (17.5 divided by 5) equals one pound of flour by weight. More importantly, I like the size loaf I get when I use 3-1/2 vs. 3 cups flour in both size bread pans. And, I find 3 cups flour ideal for raisin bread in the smaller 8" x 4" pan.

Bottom-line, it's personal preference. One loaf is a little taller and the other is a little wider... what size sandwich do you want? You're the baker... you decide.

Testing the Options

The concept of using a PMDO. to bake sandwich bread is a new technique, thus I felt it was important to test the options. While testing bread pans for this cookbook, I didn't learn anything that was earth-shaking, but I did learn some good general rules. Here are the pans I tested and a few observations.

Note: The description of the pans—like all the others—was taken from the manufacture's marketing material.

Good Cook 8" x 4" Loaf Pan
Description: 8" x 4" x 2-1/4" professional gauge steel nonstick small loaf pan

Liquid Capacity: 42 oz | Its liquid capacity is 6 ounces less (42 vs. 48) than the typical 8-1/2" x 4-1/2" loaf pan and 3-1/2 cups flour is just a little too much, thus I favor recipes using 3 cups for this size pan.

Fastener: Medium binder clips

Recommended... *Good Cook* is the brand frequently found in grocery stores. It's inexpensive, an excellent value and ideal for home use. I was very pleased with the performance of the pans. They did an excellent job baking the crumb and developing the crust, fit was snug, binder clips were easy to attach and remove, and the unit was stable.

This is my "go-to" pan for raisin bread when I want a smaller loaf.

Mainstays 8.4" x 4.4" Cheap Loaf Pan
Description: 8.4" x 4.4" x 2.5" light weight loaf pan

Liquid Capacity: 44 oz

Fastener: Medium binder clips

Not recommended... this loaf pan is one step above foil. It has its uses, but bread making isn't one of them. The internal temperature of this loaf was over 200 degrees F, but the crust didn't develop. Light colored, light weight, metal is not well suited for bread baking. It only cost a few dollars more to get a quality pan... it's worth the money.

Wilton 8-1/2" x 4-1/2" Loaf Pan
Description: 8-1/2" x 4-1/2" x 2-1/2" heavy gage steel nonstick loaf pan

Liquid Capacity: 46 oz | The opening is not a true 8-1/2" x 4-1/2" and the sides are more tapered, thus its liquid capacity is less than others. It size is borderline between recipes using 3 or 3-1/2 cups flour. Because of its lower liquid capacity, it can be used in place of the 8" x 4" bread pan.

Fastener: Large binder clips

Recommended... *Wilton* is well known for their bakeware (specifically cake bakeware) and they make quality bread pans. They did an excellent job baking the crumb and developing the crust, the clips were easy to attach and remove, and the unit was very stable.

American Bakeware 8-1/2" x 4-1/2" Loaf Pan
Description: 8-1/2" x 4-1/2" x 2-3/4" heavy gage loaf pan reinforced with titanium for superior release and easy cleanup

Liquid Capacity: 48 oz

Fastener: Large binder clips

Recommended… the *American Bakeware* loaf pan has the largest handles and widest rim. They did an excellent job baking the crumb and developing the crust, fit was snug, the clips were easy to attach and remove, and the unit was very stable.

Lodge 8-1/2" x 4-1/2" Cast Iron Loaf Pan
Description: 8-1/2" x 4-1/2" x 2-1/2" pre-seasoned cast iron loaf pan

Liquid Capacity: 48 oz

Fastener: None... the pans have a nice wide flat rim and top pan rested securely on the bottom pan without clips.

Others are better... I like *Lodge*, but the thickness and weight of the cast iron was a problem. The internal temperature was 200+ degrees F (just like the others), the crust was okay, but the top sagged. The unit was sung, stable, and easy to handle without binder clips, but the others made a better loaf.

Note: I did test preheated cast iron loaf pans... the loaf was excellent, but not worth the effort.

Chicago Metallic 8-1/2" x 4-1/2" Loaf Pan
Description: 8-1/2" x 4-1/2" x 2-3/4" 26 gage aluminized steel diamond-quality nonstick loaf pan

Liquid Capacity: 48 oz

Fastener: None... I balanced the top on the bottom, but it would have been nice to have a flat rim and handles. If it is important to you to secure the top you can use silicone cooking bands or food ties.

Good... *Chicago Metallic* makes excellent bakeware. It's the workhorse found in many professional kitchens because of its heavy gage metal construction and excellent non-stick surface. They're excellent for home and professional use. They did an excellent job baking the crumb and developing the crust. I balanced one pan on top of the other and it worked just fine. They are a little harder to clean because of the square corners.

Chicago Metallic and *USA* are very similar in size and performance.

USA 8-1/2" x 4-1/2" Loaf Pan
Description: 8-1/2" x 4-1/2" x 2-3/4" heavy gage aluminized steel loaf pan

Liquid Capacity: 48 oz

Fastener: Silicone cooking bands

Good... *USA* makes excellent bakeware. It's the workhorse found in many professional kitchens because of its heavy gage metal construction and excellent non-stick surface. They're excellent for home and professional use. It did an excellent job baking the crumb and developing the crust. I couldn't balance one pan on top of the other so I use silicone bands. They are a little harder to clean because of the square corners.

USA and *Chicago Metallic* are very similar in size and performance.

OXO Good Grips 8-1/2" x 4-1/2" Loaf Pan
Description: 9" x 5" x 2-1/2" x 2-7/8" non-stick pro 1 lb loaf pan

Liquid Capacity: 52 oz | Its liquid capacity is 4 ounces more than (52 vs. 48) *USA* and *Chicago Metallic* which wasn't really noticeable.

Fastener: Large binder clips

Best of the best… the *OXO Good Grips* loaf pans performed very well. They did an excellent job baking the crumb and developing the crust, fit was snug, binder clips were easy to attach and remove, and the unit was stable. These are my new go to PMDO.. I liked them so much I went out and bought a couple more sets for when I make batches.

Granite-Ware 9" x 5" Loaf Pan

Description: 9" x 5" x 2-1/2" steel core dark ceramic surface naturally nonstick loaf pan

Liquid Capacity: 54 oz | This was the smallest of the 9" x 5" pans with a liquid capacity 10 ounces less (54 vs. 64) than the average large loaf pans. The shape of the loaf was a little different, but there was no difference in baking time or temperature.

Fastener: Medium binder clips

Recommended... the *Granite-Ware* loaf pans performed very well. They did an excellent job baking the crumb and developing the crust, fit was snug, binder clips were easy to attach and remove, and the unit was stable.

***Anchor* 9" x 5" (1.5 qt) Glass Loaf Dish**
Description: 9" x 5" x 2-3/4" glass loaf dish

Liquid capacity: 58 oz

Fastener: Silicone cooking bands

Others are better… my wife likes glass bakeware for pie crusts, etc., but the thickness and weight of the loaf dish is a problem for a poor man's Dutch oven. The internal temperature was 200+ degrees F (just like the others), but the crust did not develop as well and the top sagged. As a unit… the top did not fit well on the bottom, the silicone loops were okay, but the unit was unstable.

SilverStone 9" x 5" Hybrid Ceramic Loaf Pan
Description: 9" x 5" x 2-3/4" ceramic coated loaf pan

Liquid capacity: 60 oz

Fastener: Large binder clips

Recommended… I was pleased with the *SilverStone* loaf pans. They did an excellent job baking the crumb and developing the crust, the clips were easy to attach and remove, and the unit was stable.

Mainstays 9" x 5" Loaf Pan
Description: 9" x 5" x 2-3/4" durable non-stick loaf pan

Liquid Capacity: 64 oz

Fastener: Medium binder clips

Recommended… *Mainstays* is the brand frequently found at Wal-Mart and I wanted to do a side-by-side comparison with the *Good Cook's* loaf pan. Bottom-line, *Mainstays* and *Good Cook* are very similar in size and performance. It's inexpensive, an excellent value (a little less than *Good Cooks*) and ideal for home use. I was very pleased with the performance of the pans. They did an excellent job baking the crumb and developing the crust, fit was snug, binder clips were easy to attach and remove, and the unit was stable… one of my "go-to" pans for sandwich bread.

Good Cook 9" x 5" Loaf Pan
Description: 9" x 5" x 2-3/4" professional gauge steel nonstick large loaf pan

Liquid Capacity: 64 oz

Fastener: Medium binder clips

Recommended... *Good Cook* is the brand frequently found in grocery stores. It's inexpensive, an excellent value and ideal for home use. I was very pleased with the performance of the pans. They did an excellent job baking the crumb and developing the crust, fit was snug, binder clips were easy to attach and remove, and the unit was stable... one of my "go-to" pans for sandwich bread.

Good Cook and *Mainstays* are very similar in size and performance.

Wilton 12" x 4-1/2" Long Loaf Pan

Description: 12" x 4-1/2" x 3-1/8" professional gauge steel nonstick long loaf pan

Liquid Capacity: 76 oz

Using standard ingredients (14 oz cool water, 1-1/2 tsp salt, 1/4 tsp instant yeast & 3-1/2 cups bread flour) baking time & temperature are…

Long loaves: 35 minutes at 400 degrees F with the top on and 5 to 15 with the top off (5 minutes less baking time with the top on).

Half loaves: 30 minutes at 400 degrees F with the top on and 5 to 15 with the top off (10 minutes less baking time with the top on).

Fastener: Large binder clips

Recommended… *Wilton* long loaf pans are ideally suited for long and half loaves. They did an excellent job baking the crumb and developing the crust, fit was snug, binder clips were easy to attach and remove, and the unit was stable. It's worth having a couple of these around the house.

Conclusions

After experimenting with variety of bread pans I developed a few preferences.

Shape: I like pans with flat rims and thin handles. Flat rims... fit together better (snug) and the unit is more stable. Thin handles... allows me to use binder clips.

Metal bread pans: Metal pans were the clear winner. They heat faster and did an excellent job baking the crumb and developing the crust.

Heavy loaf pans: Loaf pans made of glass and cast iron did not fare as well. The internal temperature was 200+ degrees F (just like the others), but the crust did not develop as well and the top had a tendency to sag.

Snug fit: A snug fit between the pans is important, but it doesn't have to be air tight.

Rounded corners: Sometimes little things make a difference. After washing the bread pans I found I liked rounded corners... it's easier to clean the corners.

Size: When the recipe calls for 3 cups flour I use small bread pans (8" x 4"). When the recipes uses 3-1/2 cups flour I use either medium (8-1/2" x 4-1/2") or large pans (9" x 5") depending on the shape I want (wider vs. taller). When the recipe uses 4 cups flour I use large pans (9" x 5").

Baking times: Generally speaking, baking times for recipes using 3 cups flour are 35 minutes, 3-1/2 cups are 40 minutes, and 4 cups are 45 minutes. Long loaf pans are 5 minutes less because the loaves are thinner... less dense. And heavy ingredients (raisins, olives, etc.) need to be baked 5 to 10 minutes longer because of the moisture and mass of the ingredients.

Adjusting recipes: Each recipe (under "Options") can be adjusted to the size of your pan. The general rule of thumb is... any time you increase or decrease the amount of flour by 1/2 cup, adjust the water by 2 oz (all other ingredients remain the same) and adjust the baking time & temperature by 5 minutes with the top on.

Bread Recipes

Over the years I have worked with my readers and subscribers listening to their desires and needs… to have high quality, great tasting, fresh-from-the-oven bread that is fast, convenient, hassle-free, and reliable without special equipment or expensive bakeware. In response, I developed "hands-free" technique (dough can go straight from mixing bowl to baking vessel without touching the dough or dusting work surface with flour), "roll-to-coat" (coat dough with flour in mixing bowl… no more sticky dough), and now I've added the ability to shape no-knead dough into sandwich bread using the principles of a Dutch oven.

These techniques are a fresh approach to making no-knead bread… I think you'll love the results.

YouTube videos in support of recipe: World's Easiest No-Knead Sandwich Bread using a Poor Man's Dutch Oven demonstrates traditional method and How to Bake No-Knead Bread in a Poor Man's Dutch Oven (no mixer… no bread machine) demonstrates "Turbo" method.

Classic White Bread (PMDO | traditional method)
Classic white is the most popular bread. It's simple... it's basic. And, if you're making your first loaf... this is the place to start.

Picture: For lunch I made an egg salad sandwich... a little lettuce and my special egg salad between a couple slices of fresh-from-the-oven classic white bread. To make my special egg salad I use... 12 hard boiled eggs (sliced with a egg slicer and cut down the middle), 4 heaping tbsp mayo, 1 heaping tbsp yellow mustard, 1 heaping tbsp sweet pickle relish and a tsp salt.

Option:
"Turbo" method... if you wish to reduce the proofing time from 8 hours to 1-1/2 hours... increase yeast from 1/4 to 1-1/4 tsp and proof in a warm draft free environment (78 to 85 degrees F).

Classic White Bread

Pour water into a 3 to 4 qt glass mixing bowl.
> 14 oz cool Water

Add salt and yeast… give a quick stir to combine.
> 1-1/2 tsp Salt
> 1/4 tsp Instant Yeast

Add flour… stir until dough forms a shaggy ball, scrape dry flour from side of bowl, then tumble dough to combine moist flour with dry flour.
> 3-1/2 cups Bread Flour

Cover bowl with plastic wrap, place on counter, and proof for 8 to 24 hours.

8 to 24 hours later (PMDO)

When dough has risen and developed its gluten structure… spray bread pan (8-1/2" x 4-1/2" or 9" x 5") with no-stick cooking spray and set aside.

"Degas, pull and stretch"… stick handle end of a plastic spoon in the dough and stir (dough will form a sticky ball). Then, scrape side of bowl to get remainder of the dough into the sticky dough ball.

Roll dough out of bowl into bread pan.

Cover bottom bread pan with top pan and place in a warm draft-free location to proof for 30 minutes.

Before dough is fully proofed…

Move rack to lower third of oven and pre-heat to 400 degrees F.

30 minutes later

When dough has proofed and oven has come to temperature… place PMDO in oven and bake for 40 minutes with the top on.

40 minutes later

Remove top and bake for an additional 3 to 15 minutes to finish the crust.

3 to 15 minutes later

Gently turn loaf out on work surface and place on cooling rack.

Italian Sesame Bread (PMDO | "Turbo" method)

For the Italian sesame bread I used a "poor-man's-Dutch oven". It's the best of both worlds... the shape of sandwich bread using the principles of a Dutch oven. I used two 8-1/2" x 4-1/2" OXO bread pans, but 9" x 5" pans are perfectly acceptable.

Options:

Add sesame and flax seed to dough... you can create an interesting appearance, texture and flavor by adding 1 Tbsp (each) sesame and flax seeds to the dough.

"Traditional" method... this was written for, and demonstrated in, "No-Knead Bread 101" using the "Turbo" method. To convert it to the traditional method... decrease yeast from 1-1/4 tsp to 1/4 tsp and proof 8 to 24 hours.

YouTube Video in support of recipe: No-Knead Bread 101 (Includes demonstration of Sesame Seed Bread... Italian, Muffuletta, & Sandwich) (June 17, 2016 – 14:23)

Italian Sesame Bread

Pour warm water in a 3 to 4 qt warm glass mixing bowl (use a warm bowl... you don't want a cold bowl to take the heat out of the warm water).

    14 oz warm Water

Add salt, yeast and olive oil... give a quick stir to combine.

    1-1/2 tsp Salt
    1-1/4 tsp Instant Yeast
    1 Tbsp Extra Virgin Olive Oil
    1 Tbsp Sesame Seeds (optional)
    1 Tbsp Flax Seeds (optional)

Add flour... stir until dough forms a shaggy ball, scrape dry flour from side of bowl, then tumble dough to combine moist flour with dry flour.

    3-1/2 cups Bread Flour

Cover bowl with plastic wrap, place in a warm draft-free location, and proof for 1-1/2 hours.

1-1/2 hours later (PMDO | garnish)

When dough has risen and developed its gluten structure... spray bread pan (8-1/2" x 4-1/2" or 9" x 5") with no-stick cooking spray and set aside.

"Degas, pull and stretch"... stick handle end of a plastic spoon in the dough and stir (dough will form a sticky ball). Then, scrape side of bowl to get remainder of the dough into the sticky dough ball.

When dough has risen and developed its gluten structure... spray bottom pan with no-stick spray and set aside.

Garnish... sprinkle dough ball and side of bowl with sesame seeds, and roll-to-coat (roll dough ball in seeds to coat).

    2 Tbsp Sesame Seeds

Roll dough out of bowl into bread pan.

Cover bottom bread pan with top pan and place in a warm draft-free location to proof for 30 minutes.

Before dough is fully proofed...

Move rack to lower third of oven and pre-heat to 400 degrees F.

30 minutes later

When dough has proofed and oven has come to temperature... place PMDO in oven and bake for 40 minutes with the top on.

40 minutes later

Take pans out of the oven, remove the top, and place pan back in the oven for 3 to 15 minutes to finish the crust.

3 to 15 minutes later

Gently turn loaf out on work surface and place on cooling rack.

Cheddar Cheese Bread (PMDO)

Fresh-from-the-oven bread is special... add cheese and you have a winner. Something your friends and guests will love. This is a remarkably simple recipe that everyone is sure to enjoy.

Picture: For lunch I made a cheese sandwich. I spread mayo and yellow mustard on two slices fresh-from-the-oven cheddar cheese bread, added two slices of cheddar, two slices Swiss, one slice provolone cheese.

Option:

"Turbo" method... if you wish to reduce the proofing time from 8 hours to 1-1/2 hours... increase yeast from 1/4 to 1-1/4 tsp and proof in a warm draft free environment (78 to 85 degrees F).

Cheddar Cheese Bread

Pour water into a 3 to 4 qt glass mixing bowl.

    16 oz cool Water

Add salt and yeast... give a quick stir to combine.

    1-1/2 tsp Salt
    1/4 tsp Instant Yeast

Add flour... then cheese (if cheese is added before flour it will be harder to combine)... stir until dough forms a shaggy ball, scrape dry flour from side of bowl, then tumble dough to combine moist flour with dry flour.

    3-1/2 cups Bread Flour
    1 cup coarsely shredded Cheddar Cheese

Cover bowl with plastic wrap, place on counter, and proof for 8 to 24 hours.

8 to 24 hours later (PMDO)

When dough has risen and developed its gluten structure... spray bread pan (8-1/2" x 4-1/2" or 9" x 5") with no-stick cooking spray and set aside.

"Degas, pull and stretch"... stick handle end of a plastic spoon in the dough and stir (dough will form a sticky ball). Then, scrape side of bowl to get remainder of the dough into the sticky dough ball.

Roll dough out of bowl into bread pan.

Cover bottom bread pan with top pan and place in a warm draft-free location to proof for 30 minutes.

Before dough is fully proofed...

Move rack to lower third of oven and pre-heat to 400 degrees F.

30 minutes later

When dough has proofed and oven has come to temperature... place PMDO in oven and bake for 40 minutes with the top on.

40 minutes later

Remove top and bake for an additional 3 to 15 minutes to finish the crust.

3 to 15 minutes later

Gently turn loaf out on work surface and place on cooling rack.

Multigrain Country White Bread (PMDO)

If you haven't made multigrain bread before, this is an excellent choice for your first loaf. Simple recipe... simple flavors... universally pleasing taste. In fact, it's one of my most popular loaves. My first multigrain loaves used 2 cups bread flour and 1 cup wheat flour. One time I forgot the wheat flour and used 3 cups bread flour. Surprise, surprise, surprise... the multigrain country white became one of my most popular breads. I had assumed those who liked grains also liked wheat breads, but there appears to be a significant segment of our society who likes multigrain bread without the wheat bread taste. Wheat is one of those things you either like or don't like, but it doesn't mean you don't like multigrain bread.

Picture: For lunch I made a tuna salad sandwich... a little lettuce cupped to hold the tuna salad between a couple slices of fresh-from-the-oven multigrain country white bread. My tuna salad is made of... 1 can (12 oz) chunk light tuna in oil (drain the oil), 2 heaping tbsp mayo, 2 heaping tsp sweet pickle relish and 1 heaping tsp yellow mustard.

Option:
"Turbo" method... if you wish to reduce the proofing time from 8 hours to 1-1/2 hours... increase yeast from 1/4 to 1-1/4 tsp and proof in a warm draft free environment (78 to 85 degrees F).

Multigrain Country White Bread

Pour water into a 3 to 4 qt glass mixing bowl.
>16 oz cool Water

Add salt, yeast and seeds... give a quick stir to combine.
>1-1/2 tsp Salt
>1/4 tsp Instant Yeast
>1 Tbsp Sesame Seeds
>1 Tbsp Flax Seeds

Add flour... then oats (if oats are added before flour they will absorb the water and it will be harder to combine)... stir until dough forms a shaggy ball, scrape dry flour from side of bowl, then tumble dough to combine moist flour with dry flour.
>3-1/2 cups Bread Flour
>1/2 cup Old Fashioned Quaker Oats

Cover bowl with plastic wrap, place on counter, and proof for 8 to 24 hours.

8 to 24 hours later (PMDO)

When dough has risen and developed its gluten structure... spray bread pan (8-1/2" x 4-1/2" or 9" x 5") with no-stick cooking spray and set aside.

"Degas, pull and stretch"... stick handle end of a plastic spoon in the dough and stir (dough will form a sticky ball). Then, scrape side of bowl to get remainder of the dough into the sticky dough ball.

Roll dough out of bowl into bread pan.

Cover bottom bread pan with top pan and place in a warm draft-free location to proof for 30 minutes.

Before dough is fully proofed...

Move rack to lower third of oven and pre-heat to 400 degrees F.

30 minutes later

When dough has proofed and oven has come to temperature... place PMDO in oven and bake for 40 minutes with the top on.

40 minutes later

Remove top and bake for an additional 3 to 15 minutes to finish the crust.

3 to 15 minutes later

Gently turn loaf out on work surface and place on cooling rack.

Beer Bread (small PMDO)

There are two basic types of beer bread... yeasted and quick. Yeasted beer bread uses yeast as a leavening agent. Quick beer bread uses self rising flour which has baking soda and baking powder as leavening agents. Quick beer bread is—as the name implies—very quick and easy, but don't let that fool you. It makes delicious rolls. To see the difference between yeasted and quick you may want to watch, Introduction to No-Knead Beer Bread (a.k.a. Artisan Yeast Beer Bread) and Introduction to Quick Beer Bread (a.k.a. Beer Bread Dinner Rolls). I used two undersized *Wilton* 8-1/2" x 4-1/2" bread pans for my PMDO.

Picture: For lunch I made a stadium bratwurst & bacon sandwich. I spread mayo and yellow mustard on two slices fresh-from-the-oven beer bread, sliced the bratwursts in half (1-1/2 brats per sandwich), topped it with a slice of bacon and, of course, I had it with beer.

Options:
Larger loaf... use 3-1/2 vs. 3 cups flour, increase beer by 2 oz and increase baking time with the top on by 5 minutes.
"Turbo" method... if you wish to reduce the proofing time from 8 hours to 1-1/2 hours... increase yeast from 1/4 to 1-1/4 tsp and proof in a warm draft free environment (78 to 85 degrees F).

Beer Bread

Pour room temperature beer into a 3 to 4 qt glass mixing bowl.
>12 oz room temperature Beer

Add yeast... give a quick stir to combine.
>1/4 tsp Instant Yeast

Add salt (salt will foam)... give a quick stir to combine.
>1-1/2 tsp Salt

Add flour... stir until dough forms a shaggy ball, scrape dry flour from side of bowl, then tumble dough to combine moist flour with dry flour.
>3 cups Bread Flour

Cover bowl with plastic wrap, place on counter, and proof for 8 to 24 hours.

8 to 24 hours later (small PMDO)

When dough has risen and developed its gluten structure... spray bread pan (8" x 4" or under sized 8-1/2" x 4-1/2") with no-stick cooking spray and set aside.
"Degas, pull and stretch"... stick handle end of a plastic spoon in the dough and stir (dough will form a sticky ball). Then, scrape side of bowl to get remainder of the dough into the sticky dough ball.
Roll dough out of bowl into bread pan.
Cover bottom bread pan with top pan and place in a warm draft-free location to proof for 30 minutes.

Before dough is fully proofed...

Move rack to lower third of oven and pre-heat to 400 degrees F.

30 minutes later

When dough has proofed and oven has come to temperature... place PMDO in oven and bake for 35 minutes with the top on.

35 minutes later

Remove top and bake for an additional 3 to 15 minutes to finish the crust.

3 to 15 minutes later

Gently turn loaf out on work surface and place on cooling rack.

Honey Oatmeal Bread (PMDO)
Fresh-from-the-oven bread with the wholesome goodness of oats and the sweetness of honey… what's not to like? This loaf is as delicious to eat as it is pleasing to the eye.

Picture: For lunch I made a country fried steak sandwich… I spread mayo on two slices fresh-from-the-oven honey oatmeal bread and added 1 precook country fried steak, lettuce and tomato. Simple… surprisingly delicious.

Option:
"Turbo" method… if you wish to reduce the proofing time from 8 hours to 1-1/2 hours… increase yeast from 1/4 to 1-1/4 tsp and proof in a warm draft free environment (78 to 85 degrees F).

Honey Oatmeal Bread

Pour water into a 3 to 4 qt glass mixing bowl.
> 16 oz cool Water

Add salt, yeast and honey... give a quick stir to combine.
> 1-1/2 tsp Salt
> 1/4 tsp Instant Yeast
> 1 Tbsp Honey

Add flour... then oats (if oats are added before flour they will absorb the water and it will be harder to combine)... stir until dough forms a shaggy ball, scrape dry flour from side of bowl, then tumble dough to combine moist flour with dry flour.
> 3-1/2 cups Bread Flour
> 1 cup Old Fashioned Quaker Oats

Cover bowl with plastic wrap, place on counter, and proof for 8 to 24 hours.

8 to 24 hours later (PMDO | garnish)

When dough has risen and developed its gluten structure... spray bread pan (8-1/2" x 4-1/2" or 9" x 5") with no-stick cooking spray and set aside.

"Degas, pull and stretch"... stick handle end of a plastic spoon in the dough and stir (dough will form a sticky ball). Then, scrape side of bowl to get remainder of the dough into the sticky dough ball.

Garnish... sprinkle dough ball and side of bowl with oats, and roll-to-coat (roll dough ball in oats to coat).
> 1/4 cup Old Fashioned Quaker Oats

Roll dough out of bowl into bread pan.

Cover bottom bread pan with top pan and place in a warm draft-free location to proof for 30 minutes.

Before dough is fully proofed...

Move rack to lower third of oven and pre-heat to 400 degrees F.

30 minutes later

When dough has proofed and oven has come to temperature... place PMDO in oven and bake for 40 minutes with the top on.

40 minutes later

Remove top and bake for an additional 3 to 15 minutes to finish the crust.

3 to 15 minutes later

Gently turn loaf out on work surface and place on cooling rack.

Honey Whole Wheat Bread (PMDO)
This whole wheat recipe balances the nutrition and nutty taste of whole wheat with the crumb of a Country White in a hearty, moist loaf with a touch of honey for sweetness.

Picture: For lunch I made a deli-fresh turkey, ham and cheese sandwich. I spread mayo on two slices fresh-from-the-oven honey whole wheat bread, added several slices of turkey and ham, then topped it with lettuce and tomato, and I put provolone cheese on one and Swiss on the other.

Option:
"Turbo" method... if you wish to reduce the proofing time from 8 hours to 1-1/2 hours... increase yeast from 1/4 to 1-1/4 tsp and proof in a warm draft free environment (78 to 85 degrees F).

Honey Whole Wheat Bread

Pour water into a 3 to 4 qt glass mixing bowl.
> 16 oz cool Water

Add salt, yeast, olive oil and honey... give a quick stir to combine.
> 1-1/2 tsp Salt
> 1/4 tsp Instant Yeast
> 1 Tbsp extra-virgin Olive Oil
> 1 Tbsp Honey

Add flour... stir until dough forms a shaggy ball, scrape dry flour from side of bowl, then tumble dough to combine moist flour with dry flour.
> 1-1/2 cups Bread Flour
> 2 cups Whole Wheat Flour

Cover bowl with plastic wrap, place on counter, and proof for 8 to 24 hours.

8 to 24 hours later (PMDO)

When dough has risen and developed its gluten structure... spray bread pan (8-1/2" x 4-1/2" or 9" x 5") with no-stick cooking spray and set aside.

"Degas, pull and stretch"... stick handle end of a plastic spoon in the dough and stir (dough will form a sticky ball). Then, scrape side of bowl to get remainder of the dough into the sticky dough ball.

Roll dough out of bowl into bread pan.

Cover bottom bread pan with top pan and place in a warm draft-free location to proof for 30 minutes.

Before dough is fully proofed...

Move rack to lower third of oven and pre-heat to 400 degrees F.

30 minutes later

When dough has proofed and oven has come to temperature... place PMDO in oven and bake for 40 minutes with the top on.

40 minutes later

Remove top and bake for an additional 3 to 15 minutes to finish the crust.

3 to 15 minutes later

Gently turn loaf out on work surface and place on cooling rack.

Harvest 8 Grain Whole Wheat Bread (PMDO)
This Harvest 8 Grain Wheat Bread has a more robust and complex flavor than the multigrain country white and wheat breads. I experimented with and tested a number of my own multigrain mixtures before discovering King Arthur's Harvest Grains Blend and (as they state on their website) the whole oat berries, millet, rye flakes and wheat flakes enhance texture while the flax, poppy, sesame, and sunflower seeds add crunch and great, nutty flavor. Wow, the flavor is great... and it's a lot easier and... more practical... to purchase a blend of seeds. You should experiment with blends available in your community.

Because whole wheat loaves can be a little too heavy and dense for some tastes... I like to balance the nutritional value of whole wheat with the crumb and texture of bread flour by using a blend.

Picture: For lunch I made a roast beef & bacon sandwich. I spread mayo on two slices fresh-from-the-oven harvest 8 grain whole wheat bread, added lettuce, sliced roast beef, and a couple slices of bacon.

Option:
"Turbo" method... if you wish to reduce the proofing time from 8 hours to 1-1/2 hours... increase yeast from 1/4 to 1-1/4 tsp and proof in a warm draft free environment (78 to 85 degrees F).

Harvest 8 Grain Whole Wheat Bread

Pour water into a 3 to 4 qt glass mixing bowl.
>18 oz cool Water

Add salt, yeast, olive oil and grains... give a quick stir to combine.
>1-1/2 tsp Salt
>1/4 tsp Instant Yeast
>1 Tbsp extra-virgin Olive Oil
>2/3 cup King Arthur Harvest Grains Blend

Add flour... stir until dough forms a shaggy ball, scrape dry flour from side of bowl, then tumble dough to combine moist flour with dry flour.
>1-1/2 cups Bread Flour
>2 cups Whole Wheat Flour

Cover bowl with plastic wrap, place on counter, and proof for 8 to 24 hours.

8 to 24 hours later (PMDO | garnish & baste)

When dough has risen and developed its gluten structure... spray bread pan (8-1/2" x 4-1/2" or 9" x 5") with no-stick cooking spray and set aside.

"Degas, pull and stretch"... stick handle end of a plastic spoon in the dough and stir (dough will form a sticky ball). Then, scrape side of bowl to get remainder of the dough into the sticky dough ball.

Garnish... sprinkle dough ball and side of bowl with grains, and roll-to-coat (roll dough ball in grains to coat).
>2 Tbsp King Arthur Harvest Grains Blend

Baste (optional)... place 1 egg yolk in a small mixing bowl, add water, and whip with a fork to combine. Then pour egg wash into mixing bowl and roll-to-coat.
>1 lg Egg Yolk
>1 tsp Water

Roll dough out of bowl into bread pan.

Cover bottom bread pan with top pan and place in a warm draft-free location to proof for 30 minutes.

Before dough is fully proofed...

Move rack to lower third of oven and pre-heat to 400 degrees F.

30 minutes later

When dough has proofed and oven has come to temperature... place PMDO in oven and bake for 40 minutes with the top on.

40 minutes later

Remove top and bake for an additional 3 to 15 minutes to finish the crust.

3 to 15 minutes later

Gently turn loaf out on work surface and place on cooling rack.

Deli Rye Bread (PMDO)
This is a rustic rye bread, with a mild rye flavor and a generous amount of caraway seeds that would be the perfect complement to a pastrami sandwich.

Picture: For lunch I made a simple pastrami sandwich. I spread mayo and yellow mustard on two slices fresh-from-the-oven deli rye bread and added 5 slices of pastrami.

YouTube Video in support of recipe: World's Easiest No-Knead Deli Rye Bread (no mixer… "hands-free" technique) (July 2016 - 6:51)

Options:
Larger loaf… use 3-1/2 vs. 3 cups flour, increase water by 2 oz and increase baking time with the top on by 5 minutes.
"Turbo" method… if you wish to reduce the proofing time from 8 hours to 1-1/2 hours… increase yeast from 1/4 to 1-1/4 tsp and proof in a warm draft free environment (78 to 85 degrees F).

Deli Rye Bread

Pour water into a 3 to 4 qt glass mixing bowl.
>14 oz cool Water

Add salt, yeast, sugar, olive oil and seeds... give a quick stir to combine.
>1-1/2 tsp Salt
>1/2 tsp Instant Yeast
>1 Tbsp Sugar
>2 Tbsp Caraway Seeds
>1 Tbsp extra-virgin Olive Oil

Add flour... stir until dough forms a shaggy ball, scrape dry flour from side of bowl, then tumble dough to combine moist flour with dry flour.
>2-1/2 cups Bread Flour
>1 cup Rye Flour

Cover bowl with plastic wrap, place on counter, and proof for 8 to 24 hours.

8 to 24 hours later (PMDO)

When dough has risen and developed its gluten structure... spray bread pan (8-1/2" x 4-1/2" or 9" x 5") with no-stick cooking spray and set aside.

"Degas, pull and stretch"... stick handle end of a plastic spoon in the dough and stir (dough will form a sticky ball). Then, scrape side of bowl to get remainder of the dough into the sticky dough ball.

Roll dough out of bowl into bread pan.

Cover bottom bread pan with top pan and place in a warm draft-free location to proof for 30 minutes.

Before dough is fully proofed...

Move rack to lower third of oven and pre-heat to 400 degrees F.

30 minutes later

When dough has proofed and oven has come to temperature... place PMDO in oven and bake for 40 minutes with the top on.

40 minutes later

Remove top and bake for an additional 3 to 15 minutes to finish the crust.

3 to 15 minutes later

Gently turn loaf out on work surface and place on cooling rack.

Buttermilk Bread (small PMDO)

If you like buttermilk ranch dressing... you'll like buttermilk bread. And this isn't the average buttermilk bread... this is an artisan loaf with an airy crumb and tender crust. The appearance is excellent... the taste is great. Buttermilk is a great all-purpose bread. Buttermilk gives it a rich tangy flavor with a subtle buttery depth that is great for sandwiches and toast.

It is a common misconception to associate buttermilk with the richness of butter but... buttermilk does not have butterfat. Buttermilk is the liquid remaining after taking the butter fat out of the milk in the process of making butter, thus it is lower in calories and fat than butter and higher in calcium, vitamin B12 and potassium than regular milk. And it's important to use cultured buttermilk, if you substitute 2% for cultured buttermilk in this recipe it will upset the balance of wet and dry ingredients (it's thinner), and you don't want to lose the nutritional value of buttermilk. After all, you wouldn't want to take the "yo" out of yogurt.

I used two undersized *Wilton* 8-1/2" x 4-1/2" bread pans for my PMDO.

Note: The recipe uses 1 tsp (versus 1/4) instant yeast because dairy products, like buttermilk, retard yeast activity.

Picture: For lunch I made a deli-fresh turkey sandwich. I spread mayo on two slices fresh-from-the-oven buttermilk bread, added deli-fresh turkey, lettuce and a slice of tomato.

Buttermilk Bread

Pour buttermilk and water to a 3 to 4 qt glass mixing bowl.
> 8 oz Cultured Buttermilk
> 6 oz cool Water

Add salt, yeast, sugar and oil... give a quick stir to combine.
> 1-1/2 tsp Salt
> 1 tsp Instant Yeast
> 1 Tbsp Sugar
> 1 Tbsp Vegetable Oil

Add flour... stir until dough forms a shaggy ball, scrape dry flour from side of bowl, then tumble dough to combine moist flour with dry flour.
> 3 cups Bread Flour

Cover bowl with plastic wrap, place on counter, and proof for 8 to 24 hours.

8 to 24 hours later (small PMDO | garnish)

When dough has risen and developed its gluten structure... spray bread pan (8" x 4") with no-stick cooking spray and set aside.

"Degas, pull and stretch"... stick handle end of a plastic spoon in the dough and stir (dough will form a sticky ball). Then, scrape side of bowl to get remainder of the dough into the sticky dough ball.

Garnish... sprinkle dough ball and side of bowl with sesame seeds, and roll-to-coat (roll dough ball in seeds to coat).
> 2 Tbsp Sesame Seeds

Roll dough out of bowl into bread pan.

Cover bottom bread pan with top pan and place in a warm draft-free location to proof for 30 minutes.

Before dough is fully proofed...

Move rack to lower third of oven and pre-heat to 400 degrees F.

30 minutes later

When dough has proofed and oven has come to temperature... place PMDO in oven and bake for 35 minutes with the top on.

35 minutes later

Remove top and bake for an additional 3 to 15 minutes to finish the crust.

3 to 15 minutes later

Gently turn loaf out on work surface and place on cooling rack.

Garlic Bread (long PMDO)
All of us like garlic cheese bread… I like to lightly infuse the garlic into the loaf. It gives the loaf a nice full flavor and it's easier than adding garlic after the fact.

Note: This recipe calls for 1 to 2 heaping tsp minced garlic (jar). I generally use 1, but it's a personal taste issue. Try both and see which you like.

I used two *Wilton* 12" x 4-1/2" long bread pans for my PMDO.

Picture: As an appetizer for dinner I served garlic cheese bread. Because the garlic is already infused in the bread, all I needed to do was… toast two slices, spread on a little butter, add a little cheese, a sprinkle of salt, and broil them in the toaster oven to melt the cheese.

Options:
Standard vs. long loaf pan… use the same ingredients and increase baking time with the top on by 5 minutes.
"Turbo" method… if you wish to reduce the proofing time from 8 hours to 1-1/2 hours… increase yeast from 1/4 to 1-1/4 tsp and proof in a warm draft free environment (78 to 85 degrees F).

Garlic Bread
Pour water into a 3 to 4 qt glass mixing bowl.
>14 oz cool Water

Add salt, yeast, garlic and olive oil... give a quick stir to combine.
>1-1/2 tsp Salt
>1/4 tsp Instant Yeast
>1 to 2 heaping tsp Minced Garlic (jar)
>1 Tbsp extra-virgin Olive Oil

Add flour... stir until dough forms a shaggy ball, scrape dry flour from side of bowl, then tumble dough to combine moist flour with dry flour.
>3-1/2 cups Bread Flour

Cover bowl with plastic wrap, place on counter, and proof for 8 to 24 hours.

8 to 24 hours later (long PMDO | dust with flour)
When dough has risen and developed its gluten structure... spray bread pan (12" x 4-1/2") with no-stick cooking spray and set aside.

"Degas, pull and stretch"... stick handle end of a plastic spoon in the dough and stir (dough will form a sticky ball). Then, scrape side of bowl to get remainder of the dough into the sticky dough ball.

Dust with flour... sprinkle dough ball and side of bowl with flour and roll-to-coat (dusting dough ball with flour will make it easier to handle and shape the dough for the baker).
>2 Tbsp Bread Flour

Dust work surface with flour, roll dough (and excess flour) out of bowl onto work surface, roll dough on work surface in flour to shape, and place in long PMDO.

Cover bottom bread pan with top pan and place in a warm draft-free location to proof for 30 minutes.

Before dough is fully proofed...
Move rack to lower third of oven and pre-heat to 400 degrees F.

30 minutes later
When dough has proofed and oven has come to temperature... place PMDO in oven and bake for 35 minutes with the top on.

35 minutes later
Remove top and bake for an additional 3 to 15 minutes to finish the crust.

3 to 15 minutes later
Gently turn loaf out on work surface and place on cooling rack.

Mediterranean Olive Bread (PMDO)

If a restaurant served you this loaf as their signature bread... you'd be talking about it for years and you'd be surprised how easy it is to make. I increased the baking time with the top on by 5 minutes (45 vs. 40 for a long bread pan) because the olives added mass and moisture.

Options:

Half-loaves... use two sets of long loaf pans (12" x 4-1/2"), dust with flour (roll-to-coat), divide dough in half, shape, and bake at 400 degrees for 35 minutes with the top on and 3 to 5 with the top off.

"Turbo" method... if you wish to reduce the proofing time from 8 hours to 1-1/2 hours... increase yeast from 1/4 to 1-1/4 tsp and proof in a warm draft free environment (78 to 85 degrees F).

Mediterranean Olive Bread

Prepare flavor ingredients... zest lemon, open black olives, slice green olives and kalamata olives in half, and set flavor ingredients aside.

> Zest of 1 Lemon
> 1/4 cup (2-1/4 oz can) sliced Black Olives
> 1/4 cup stuffed Green Olives (use black olive can to measure)
> 1/4 cup pitted Kalamata Olives (use black olive can to measure)

Pour water into a 3 to 4 qt glass mixing bowl.

> 14 oz cool Water

Add salt, yeast, thyme and olive oil... give a quick stir to combine.

> 1-1/2 tsp Salt
> 1/4 tsp Instant Yeast
> 1 tsp dried Thyme
> 1 Tbsp extra-virgin Olive Oil

Add flour... then flavor ingredients. Stir until dough forms a shaggy ball, scrape dry flour from side of bowl, then tumble dough to combine moist flour with dry flour.

> 3-1/2 cups Bread Flour
> Flavor ingredients (above)

Cover bowl with plastic wrap, place on counter, and proof for 8 to 24 hours.

8 to 24 hours later (PMDO)

When dough has risen and developed its gluten structure... spray bread pan (8-1/2" x 4-1/2" or 9" x 5") with no-stick cooking spray and set aside.

"Degas, pull and stretch"... stick handle end of a plastic spoon in the dough and stir (dough will form a sticky ball). Then, scrape side of bowl to get remainder of the dough into the sticky dough ball.

Roll dough out of bowl into bread pan.

Cover bottom bread pan with top pan and place in a warm draft-free location to proof for 30 minutes.

Before dough is fully proofed...

Move rack to lower third of oven and pre-heat to 400 degrees F.

30 minutes later

When dough has proofed and oven has come to temperature... place PMDO in oven and bake for 45 minutes with the top on.

45 minutes later

Remove top and bake for an additional 3 to 15 minutes to finish the crust.

3 to 15 minutes later

Gently turn loaf out on work surface and place on cooling rack.

Country White Bread (PMDO in a toaster oven)
No oven... no problem... you can bake no-knead bread in a toaster oven. This technique is ideal for those with limited kitchens and those of you who don't want to turn the oven on because it heats the house in the summer. This technique is effective with a PMDO (8-1/2" x 4-1/2" and 9" x 5") and *Sassafras* superstone oblong covered baker (13-1/2" x 4-1/2").

YouTube videos in support of recipe: "How to Bake No-Knead Bread in a Toaster Oven (no mixer... no bread machine... "hands-free" technique)"

Note:
The ideal proofing temperature is 78 to 85 degrees F, but most of our homes are 68 to 73 degrees. So... to create a favorable proofing environment I place the bowl under my desk lamp where the plastic wrap on the bowl traps the heat and raise the temperature inside the bowl to a little over 80 degrees (solar affect).

Option:
Traditional method... if you wish to use the traditional method... decrease yeast from 1-1/4 tsp to 1/4 tsp and proof 8 to 24 hours.

Country White Bread

Pour warm water in a 3 to 4 qt warm glass mixing bowl (use a warm bowl... you don't want a cold bowl to take the heat out of the warm water).

> 14 oz warm Water

Add salt and yeast... give a quick stir to combine.

> 1-1/2 tsp Salt
> 1-1/4 tsp Instant Yeast

Add flour... stir until dough forms a shaggy ball, scrape dry flour from side of bowl, then tumble dough to combine moist flour with dry flour.

> 3-1/2 cups Bread Flour

Cover bowl with plastic wrap, place bowl under a desk lamp, lower lamp so that it's close to the bowl, turn lamp on, and proof for 1-1/2 hours (see note below).

1-1/2 hours later (PMDO in a toaster oven)

When dough has risen and developed its gluten structure... spray bottom bread pan (8-1/2" x 4-1/2" or 9" x 5") with no-stick cooking spray and set aside.

"Degas, pull and stretch"... stick handle end of a plastic spoon in the dough and stir (dough will form a sticky ball). Then, scrape side of bowl to get remainder of the dough into the sticky dough ball.

Roll dough out of bowl into bread pan.

Cover bottom pan with top pan, secure with binder clips, and place PMDO in a warm draft-free location to proof for 30 minutes.

30 minutes later

Place PMDO in toaster oven, set oven to 400 degrees F, and bake for 45 minutes.

45 minutes later

Remove PMDO from oven, gently turn loaf out on to the work surface and place on cooling rack.

Cinnamon Raisin Bread (small PMDO)

Homemade fresh-from-the-oven cinnamon raisin bread is a great way to start your day and when our guests stay overnight, my wife wants them to wake up to the aroma of fresh for the oven cinnamon raisin bread filling the house.

I used two *Good Cook* 8" x 4" bread pans for my PMDO. Raisin bread is ideally suited for a smaller bread pan.

Note: This recipe has several variations... (a) I uses 1 tsp (versus 1/4 tsp) instant yeast because cinnamon retards yeast activity. (b) I increased the baking time with the top on by 10 minutes (45 versus 35 for a small bread pan) because the raisins added mass and moisture. And (c) I decreased the baking time with the top off (3 to 5 versus 5 to 15) because cinnamon raisin bread is naturally brown in color and doesn't need the extra baking time.

Picture: For breakfast we made Raisin Bread-Raspberry French Toast using fresh-from-the-oven raisin bread (next recipe).

Option:
"Turbo" method... if you wish to reduce the proofing time from 8 hours to 1-1/2 hours... increase yeast from 1 to 2-1/4 tsp yeast and proof in a warm draft free environment (78 to 85 degrees F).

Cinnamon Raisin Bread

Pour water into a 3 to 4 qt glass mixing bowl.

> 14 oz cool Water

Add salt, yeast, sugar and cinnamon... give a quick stir to combine with a flat whisk or fork (it will make it easier to combine the cinnamon).

> 1-1/2 tsp Salt
> 1 tsp Instant Yeast
> 2 Tbsp Brown Sugar
> 1 Tbsp ground Cinnamon

Add flour... then raisins. Stir until dough forms a shaggy ball, scrape dry flour from side of bowl, then tumble dough to combine moist flour with dry flour.

> 3 cups Bread Flour
> 1 cup Raisins

Cover bowl with plastic wrap, place on counter, and proof for 8 to 24 hours.

8 to 24 hours later (small PMDO)

When dough has risen and developed its gluten structure... spray bread pan (8" x 4") with no-stick cooking spray and set aside.

"Degas, pull and stretch"... stick handle end of a plastic spoon in the dough and stir (dough will form a sticky ball). Then, scrape side of bowl to get remainder of the dough into the sticky dough ball.

Roll dough out of bowl into bread pan.

Cover bottom bread pan with top pan and place in a warm draft-free location to proof for 30 minutes.

Before dough is fully proofed...

Move rack to lower third of oven and pre-heat to 400 degrees F.

30 minutes later

When dough has proofed and oven has come to temperature... place PMDO in oven and bake for 45 minutes with the top on.

45 minutes later

Remove top and bake for an additional 3 to 5 minutes to finish the crust.

3 to 5 minutes later

Gently turn loaf out on work surface and place on cooling rack.

Raisin Bread-Raspberry French Toast
This has become a recent family favorite. Try it... it's unique... it's special.

Preheat oven to 350 degrees F and spray 9" x 12" casserole dish with no-stick baking spray.
Combine milk, eggs, sugar, vanilla extract and butter in a large mixing bowl and whisk until ingredients are combined and sugar is dissolved.
      1 cups whole Milk
      4 extra large Eggs
      2/3 cups Sugar
      1 tsp Vanilla Extract
      1 Tbsp melted Butter
Cover bottom of casserole dishes with raisin bread.
      8 slices Raisin Bread
Spread milk mixture over bread and add raspberries.
      1/2 pint fresh Raspberries
Bake uncovered for 40 minutes at 350 degrees F.
Serve plain or with... maple syrup, fresh raspberries, whip cream, etc.

Made in the USA
Monee, IL
08 April 2020